George Orwell
Review of *Mein Kampf*

ERIS
gems

IT IS A SIGN OF THE SPEED AT WHICH events are moving that Hurst and Blackett's unexpurgated edition of *Mein Kampf*, published only a year ago, is edited from a pro-Hitler angle. The obvious intention of the translator's preface and notes is to tone down the book's ferocity and present Hitler in as kindly a light as possible. For at that date Hitler was still respectable. He had crushed the German labour movement, and for that the property-owning classes were willing to forgive him almost anything. Both Left and Right concurred in the very shallow notion that National Socialism was merely a version of Conservatism.

Then suddenly it turned out that Hitler was not respectable after all. As one result of this, Hurst and Blackett's edition was reissued in a new jacket explaining that all profits would be devoted to the Red Cross. Nevertheless, simply on the internal evidence of *Mein Kampf*, it is difficult to believe that any real change has taken place in Hitler's aims and opinions. When one compares his utterances of a year or so ago with those made fifteen years earlier, a thing that strikes one is the rigidity of his mind, the way in which his world-view *doesn't* develop. It is the fixed vision of a monomaniac and not likely to be much affected by the temporary manoeuvres of power politics. Probably, in Hitler's own mind, the Russo-German Pact represents no more than an alteration of timetable. The plan laid down in *Mein Kampf* was to smash Russia first, with the implied intention of smashing England afterwards. Now, as it has turned out, England has got to be dealt with first, because Russia was the more easily bribed of the two. But Russia's turn will come when England is out of the picture—that, no doubt, is how Hitler sees it. Whether it will turn out that way is of course a different question.

Suppose that Hitler's programme could be put into effect. What he envisages, a hundred years hence, is a continuous state of 250 million Germans with plenty of "living room" (i.e. stretching to Afghanistan or thereabouts), a horrible brainless empire in which, essentially, nothing ever happens except the training of young men for war and the endless breeding of fresh cannon-fodder. How was it that he was able to put this monstrous vision across? It is easy to say that at one stage of his career he was financed by the heavy industrialists, who saw in him the man who would smash the Socialists and Communists. They would not have backed him, however, if he had not talked a great movement into existence already. Again, the situation in Germany, with its seven million unemployed, was obviously favourable for demagogues. But Hitler could not have succeeded against his many rivals if it had not been for the attraction of his own personality, which one can feel even in the clumsy writing of *Mein Kampf*, and which is no doubt overwhelming when one hears his speeches. I should like to put it on record that I have never been able to dislike Hitler. Ever since he came to power—till then, like nearly everyone, I had been deceived into thinking that he did not matter—I have reflected that I would certainly kill him if I could get within reach of him, but that I could feel no personal animosity. The fact is that there is something deeply appealing about him. One feels it again when one sees his photographs—and I recommend especially the photograph at the beginning of Hurst and Blackett's edition, which shows Hitler in his early Brownshirt days. It is a pathetic, dog-like face, the face of a man suffering under intolerable wrongs. In a rather more manly way it reproduces the expression of innumerable pictures of Christ crucified, and there is little doubt that that is how Hitler sees himself. The initial, personal cause of his grievance against the universe can only be guessed at; but at any rate the grievance is here. He is the martyr, the victim, Prometheus chained to the rock, the self-sacrificing hero who fights single-handed against impossible odds. If he were killing a mouse he would know how to make it seem like a dragon. One feels, as with Napoleon, that he is fighting against destiny, that he *can't* win, and yet that he somehow deserves to. The attraction of such a pose is of course enormous; half the films that one sees turn upon some such theme.

Also he has grasped the falsity of the hedonistic attitude to life. Nearly all western thought since the last war, certainly all "progressive" thought, has assumed tacitly that human beings desire nothing beyond ease, security and avoidance of pain. In such a view of life there is no room, for instance, for patriotism and the military virtues. The Socialist who finds his children playing with soldiers is usually upset, but he is never able to think of a substitute for the tin soldiers; tin pacifists somehow won't do. Hitler, because in his own joyless mind he feels it with exceptional strength, knows that human beings *don't* only want comfort, safety, short working-hours, hygiene, birth-control and, in general, common sense; they also, at least intermittently, want struggle and self-sacrifice, not to mention drums, flags and loyalty-parades. However they may be as economic theories, Fascism and Nazism are psychologically far sounder than any hedonistic conception of life. The same is probably true of Stalin's militarised version of Socialism. All three of the great dictators have enhanced their power by imposing intolerable burdens on their peoples. Whereas Socialism, and even capitalism in a more grudging way, have said to people "I offer you a good time," Hitler has said to them "I offer you struggle, danger and death," and as a result a whole nation flings itself at his feet. Perhaps later on they will get sick of it and change their minds, as at the end of the last war. After a few years of slaughter and starvation "Greatest happiness of the greatest number" is a good slogan, but at this moment "Better an end with horror than a horror without end" is a winner. Now that we are fighting against the man who coined it, we ought not to underrate its emotional appeal.

ERIS

265 Riverside Dr. #4G
New York, NY 10025

Review of Adolph Hitler's "Mein Kampf" by George Orwell, originally published in *New English Weekly* on 21 March 1940.

ISBN 978-1-967751-22-8

All rights reserved. No part of this publication may be reproduced, stored in a retrieval system or transmitted in any form or by any means, electronic, mechanical, photocopying, recording or otherwise, without prior permission in writing from the Publisher.

eris.press